Business Acumen

How Every Leader at Ford
Can Move the Company Forward

by Ram Charan

with an introduction by Jac Nasser
President and CEO, Ford Motor Company

To the memory of Henry Ford...

whose visionary leadership
and business acumen changed the world.

BUSINESS ACUMEN

Jac Nasser with the T-Bird concept car.

INTRODUCTION

"People are drowning in information and starved for knowledge."

— John Naisbitt and Patricia Aburdene
Megatrends

I came across this quote some time ago, and while it was referring specifically to the advent of the Internet, I've often thought about it as it relates to our workdays here at Ford Motor Company.

Every day I walk into my office, as each of you does, and have e-mail, paper mail, proposals, FYIs, reports, periodicals and more awaiting my attention. The majority of it is necessary in doing the job we must do, but what I find most beneficial are the items that don't just provide me with information, but those that give me knowledge and stimulate ideas.

To that end, I'd like to present to you the first in a series of books commissioned to provide a succinct foundation of knowledge and ideas for you as leaders. There will be six books in total. Following *Business Acumen*, there will be one book devoted to each of the five areas we are leveraging for competitive advantage:

- Strong Global Brands
- Superior Customer Satisfaction & Loyalty
- Best Total Value to Consumers
- Nimble Organization with Leaders at All Levels
- Corporate Citizenship

These areas are the base of our Ford Motor Company Strategy Pyramid and our basis for success.

To start the series, I called upon my friend, esteemed adviser and renowned strategist, Ram Charan. This book has been custom-designed to help you, as a member of the Ford leadership team, develop your unique sense of business acumen. Use it to understand how successful business people — in any country, any size company — think. Many people become managers and lose sight of the simplicity and common sense of business, something they may have known in their early years.

The best businesspeople never lose sight of the common sense of business. This book is the first in the series because we must first have fundamentally the best businesspeople. Then, we will accomplish our other five objectives.

Build on your own common sense. Expand your

personal capacity as a leader of Ford Motor Company by becoming a true businessperson. And please, expand the capacity of those around you, those you lead, by sharing what you have learned, sharing your knowledge, your enthusiasm, your creativity, your commitment.

At Ford Motor Company, there are leaders at all levels. You can make a difference and drive us forward.

— Jac Nasser
Dearborn, Michigan
November 1999

PART I

THE UNIVERSAL LANGUAGE OF BUSINESS

CHAPTER 1

Be a Businessperson

Wherever you go in the world, you will see street vendors hawking goods. In Mexico City, São Paulo, Bombay, Barcelona, San Francisco, and even in Dearborn. You've probably never stopped to talk to any of them about business. But if you did, you may have noticed that these street vendors, no matter where they live, what they sell, or what culture they come from, talk about — and think about — their business in remarkably similar ways. They speak a universal language of business. They practice a universal law of business.

You may be surprised to learn that the street vendor's language is the same as Jack Welch's language (he's the CEO of General Electric Company, widely considered one of the best CEOs of our time) and Michael Dell's language (you've heard of Dell Computer) and Larry Bossidy's language (CEO of Allied Signal). It's the same as Jorma Ollila's (the CEO of Finnish company Nokia) and Niall FitzGerald's (chairman of Britain's Unilever plc).

In other words, when it comes to running a business successfully, the street vendor and the CEOs of some of the world's largest corporations talk and think very much alike. There are differences, of course, between running a huge corporation and a small shop, and we'll get to those, but the fundamentals, or basics, of **business acumen** are the

same. People like Jack Welch, Michael Dell, and Larry Bossidy manage and lead large numbers of people, but they don't think of themselves as managers. They think of themselves as businesspeople first, not unlike a street vendor.

Remember Your Roots

Many successful CEOs have had experiences early in their lives that were similar to the street vendor's, giving root to their business thinking. Jac Nasser first made his living in the restaurant business. Think of the challenges a restaurant owner faces. He has to decide location, clientele, food, price, whom to hire, and he has to put in long, long hours. If he makes money, saves some and has the right people around him, he can open a second restaurant. Every decision matters.

The restaurant business was where Jac Nasser learned the universal language of business. The same language applies to Ford, the second-largest company in the world.

Do you speak the universal language of business? Do you understand the fundamentals that underlie every business? Do you understand the basics of Ford Motor Company's business?

Chances are you've built your career in one area, or chimney, maybe sales or production. Such experience tends to narrow your perspective and influence the trade-offs you make every day. What's best for your department or function is not necessarily best for the company as a whole.

Regardless of your job, department or chimney, you as a leader must see Ford Motor Company as a *total business* and make decisions that enhance its overall performance.

You may be a top-notch professional — good at marketing or engineering or finance — but are you really a businessperson? Regardless of your job, department or chimney, you as a leader must see Ford Motor Company as a **total business** and make decisions that enhance its overall performance.

You can make a difference with this type of thinking. You also will get more excited about your job, like when you were a kid making money for the first time. Like Michael Dell, who instinctively focused on the right things and created tremendous value for shareholders. Fifteen years ago, he was running the business out of his college dorm room. By mid-1999, the market capitalization of Dell Computer was $97 billion. Ford's was $60 billion.

Let this book draw out your **business acumen**. Remember your earliest money-making experiences and build on them. Learn the universal language of business and think like a businessperson. Doing so will make your dialogue with colleagues from other functions more interesting and successful. Use this book as a guide to become a true business leader.

The Street Vendor's Skill

Can you imagine what it's like to be a street vendor hawking fruits and vegetables in a small Indian village? How does he or she make a living? Someone with a $75,000 education might say, "Anticipate demand." But the street vendor in India doesn't know the buzz words. He just has to figure out what to buy that morning — what quantity, what quality and mix of fruits and vegetables — based on what he thinks he can sell that day.

Then he has to figure out the pricing and be nimble enough to adjust it as needed during the day.

He doesn't want to carry the fruit (the inventory) home with him. If it begins to decay, it will be of less value tomorrow. Why else doesn't he want anything left over? He needs the **cash**. All day long he has to weigh whether to cut the price, when to cut it, and by how much. If he is indecisive or makes a wrong trade-off, he may lose out. Similarly, Ford Motor Company increases promotions, discounts and ads if a recession causes inventories to pile up.

Each morning, the street vendor sets up his cart. He puts the best-looking fruit in the front (retailers call this merchandising). He watches the competition — what they're selling and for how much. And the whole time, he's thinking about not just today but also tomorrow.

If he has trouble selling his things, he might have to cut the price (increase value), rearrange the display or yell louder (advertise) to attract attention to his stand. Maybe tomorrow he'll find a more successful assortment of fruits and vegetables (product mix). If something doesn't work, he adjusts. How does he know if he's doing well? If he has cash in his pocket at the end of the day. Everyone understands **cash**, money in the pocket. Every language has a word for this. The street vendor constantly thinks about **cash** — does he have enough cash, how can he get more cash, will he continue to be able to generate cash?

What happens to the street vendor who doesn't have cash at the end of the day? His family might not eat. Nothing is more powerful in focusing the mind. But he has other problems, too. How will he buy goods for the next day? He needs cash to stay in business. (Ford Motor Company went through $11 billion in the early 1990s recession.)

Our street vendor has borrowed his cash. He borrows money and uses it to make some more money. To make a living, he has to make enough money to pay back what he borrowed, with some left over.

Every time he sells a melon, he makes just a little bit of money. His profit, the difference between what he pays for the fruit and what he sells it for, is very low. His **profit margin** — the cash he gets to keep as a percentage of the total cash he takes in — is around 5 percent. (Ford calls this percentage **return on sales**. Different words, same concept.)

How vendors buy fruit varies from country to country. In India, where personal cash savings are hard to accumulate, the vendor may have to borrow money to purchase fruit.

Let's say our street vendor borrows 400 rupees (Rs. 400, which is about $10). He uses it as a deposit on Rs. 4,000 worth of fruit. If he sells all Rs. 4,000 worth of fruit at a 2 percent profit margin (after deducting all expenses and his salary), he will make a profit of Rs. 80. In other words, he used his Rs. 400 asset to make Rs. 80, so his **return on assets** is 20 percent.

Can the street vendor raise his prices to make more profit? Only so much. If his price is too high, his **customers** will go to another vendor. Can he find a way to pay less for the fruit? If he buys fruit that's overripe, his customers will know the difference. Maybe some kinds of fruit are more profitable than others. Should he sell only the most profitable ones? (In the 1980s, Ford recognized the increasing customer need for trucks, which are more profitable than cars, and changed its product mix. GM followed late.)

The street vendor has many realities to deal with. If he makes the wrong judgment repeatedly, he will find it hard to make a living. If he doesn't give his customers a fair deal, they will not return and he will develop a bad reputation. If, on the other hand, he gives people a good value every time, he builds their trust and loyalty to his brand. He is "consumer focused."

Running a one-person business may seem simple, but it requires many decisions. These judgments are made intuitively, without the benefit of computers, sophisticated forecasting techniques or coffee-drinking off-site meetings. The skill is passed down from generation to generation in cities and villages around the world, as children listen to their elders.

My experience growing up in India is typical of how children learn about business. Every evening at around 9 o'clock my male cousins and I followed my father and uncle home from their small retail apparel shop and gathered on the rooftop to escape the sweltering heat below. We discussed the day's events — what customers came or didn't come, what sold or didn't sell, whom we needed to collect money from the next morning, and what the two most prosperous shops in the village were doing (best practices). Although we didn't use the terminology, we were learning the basics of money-making and creating value for "shareholders" (the family members).

CHAPTER 2

Money-Making Basics

In 1903, Ford was one of 88 U.S. car manufacturers. But Ford was different from most competitors in one important respect: It made money from the start. Henry Ford was a businessperson.

When two businesspeople talk, whether or not they are in the same industry, whether or not they talk openly, they always try to gauge the other's business. Is her business making money? How does her business make money? Lou Gerstner didn't have a background in the computer industry when he became CEO of IBM. But he was a businessperson who understood money-making and started asking the right questions.

Money-making has three parts: **cash, return on assets,**

and **growth**. True businesspeople understand them individually as well as the relationships between them. Add **consumers** to the three parts of money-making — cash, return, growth — and you have the core, or nucleus, of any business.

> Cash, return, growth and customers. Everything else about a business emanates from this nucleus.

Cash, return, growth and customers. Everything else about a business emanates from this nucleus. Does the business generate cash and earn a good return? Are customers happy? Is the business growing? If so, common sense tells you that the business is doing well.

In today's world of large, publicly owned companies, people ask, "Does this business create shareholder value? Does it create more value for shareholders than they could earn by investing their money elsewhere?" Ford uses the concept of **shareholder value added** (SVA) as the primary metric for measuring the business. It reflects the quality of financial results and takes into account cash, return on assets, and growth. It's a kind of shorthand for judging how well the business is performing overall.

While SVA is a great single metric, it is important to

have a true understanding of the elements that help drive SVA (that is, cash, return on assets, and growth). I like to focus on these elements in my teachings, but I like Ford's thinking on SVA to bring it all together. Throughout the book, I'll talk about all of these measures.

Don't let your formal education obscure the simplicity of your business. Think like the street vendor. Cut through to the nucleus of the business. If your business shows deterioration in one or more of the basic components of money-making, use common sense to fix it. Now you are on your way to thinking like a businessperson!

Cash

Cash is one indication of money-making ability. An astute businessperson wants to know, "Does the business generate enough cash? What are the sources of cash generation? How is the cash being used?" Any businessperson who fails to ask eventually hurts himself.

Do you know whether Ford's cash is increasing or decreasing? Do you know whether Ford Automotive generates or consumes cash? (You'll get the answers later.)

There was a time when General Motors was showing better earnings every quarter when in fact its business was starting to decline. Earnings looked good because the accountants were changing the way they kept the books (legally and legitimately). A board member noticed that although earnings were improving, cash flow was turning south, and he raised the question.

Do you know the universal language of business?

- Cash
- Return on assets
- Growth
- Consumers
- Creating shareholder value
- All in the context of the changing economic landscape, marketplace, and competition

To a businessperson, cash represents the ability to stay in business. It is the oxygen supply. Most people can understand cash on a small scale, in their own everyday lives. If the bills are due before the paycheck arrives, what happens? In a large company, some people lose sight of cash. Maybe they think that's what the finance department is for.

Everybody Counts

Everyone in a company must be aware that his actions use cash or generate cash. A sales rep who negotiates a 30-day payment vs. 45 days influences cash. A plant manager whose poor planning makes overtime necessary or accumulates a lot of inventory on the floor influences cash. A decision to build a plant and never use it clearly influences cash. In the 1980s, Miller Brewing built a state-of-the-art beer plant for $460 million. The plant never opened.

Even mailroom clerks have a role to play. They sort and deliver the mail — letters, bills and checks. Checks!

Let's say the mail arrives Friday morning. The mailroom might not sort and deliver it until that afternoon. Maybe the checks don't get to the right department until 4:30. By then, the people in accounts receivable are getting ready to go home. They'll open the mail on Monday. When does the check turn into cash? Three days after it gets to the bank.

When does the mail get sent? In the 1970s, when interest rates and inflation were sky-high, American Hospital Supply discovered that invoices prepared after 2 p.m. on Friday weren't sent out until Monday morning. By getting the invoices in the mail before the end of the day Friday, the company received payments two days sooner and improved its cash situation. Lots of people keep the cash flowing, including the men and women in the mailroom.

In recent years, some very smart businesspeople have figured out highly efficient ways to generate cash. Many of these efforts focus on inventory, which ties up cash. Amazon.com, the revolutionary Internet bookseller, has a huge cash advantage over traditional booksellers, which maintain large inventories and numerous retail outlets. Instead, it receives orders through the Internet, and the books are shipped directly from the supplier to the customer. Amazon.com gets paid by the credit card company when the books are shipped. It typically pays for the books about 46 days later. The more Amazon.com grows, the more cash it generates.

Similarly, Dell Computer, which sells PCs directly to customers, gets paid on delivery. It pays suppliers in the usual 30 days and maintains just eight days of inventory. The more Dell grows, the more cash it generates.

Microsoft has a net cash flow of half a billion dollars a month. Its cost of inventory is near zero. Microsoft is a cash generating business. GE also generates a lot of cash ($10 billion in 1998). Despite a large number of acquisitions (108 last year), GE was a net cash generator.

Businesspeople know that the purpose of generating cash is to use it to grow the business. Invested wisely, cash improves the company's money-making ability. If Ford Motor Company cuts its inventories in half, it will free up a minimum of $3 billion in cash tax-free.

Return on Assets

You might think that making money simply means making a profit — buying low and selling high. But there's more.

Regardless of the size or kind of business, you're using your own or someone else's money to grow. You borrow from a bank or use your savings. That money represents your investment, or your investment capital. Maybe you inherit the business, so the "investment" is given to you.

Your investment then takes one form or another, whether it be products ("inventory"), a small store and some shelving ("plant and equipment"), or an IOU from a customer who took something home ("accounts receivable").

Even if it's not a manufacturing business, you have some investment. In the financial services or insurance business, you don't have inventories and machinery but your cash is tied up in other ways. The things you've invested in are assets.

A businessperson will wonder how much money you are able to make with those assets. What kind of money is being returned to you through their use? In short, what is your return on assets, your ROA? Are you making enough of a return on those assets?

Some people would rather talk about return on investment (ROI) or return on invested capital (ROIC). The difference is technical. How much money are you

making with the money you've invested? It's the same notion. (But it's not the same as return on sales, ROS, the language Ford typically uses for profit margin.)

You don't need an MBA to understand this notion. Let me prove the point. Many years ago I took a group of MBA students to an open-air market eight miles from Managua, Nicaragua. We stopped to talk with a woman selling apparel from a small shack. If she bought a blouse for $9.50, she could fetch about $10 for it in the market. Her profit was just 50 cents, or 5 percent of the selling price. Yet she was paying 35 percent interest on the money she borrowed.

We asked her how she could make a high enough return to pay those interest rates. Annoyed by the stupidity of the question, the woman heaved a sigh and used her right hand to make a circular motion in the air. Turning the stock over. Inventory turns. She knew that earning a good return had two ingredients — profit margin and velocity.

The word velocity describes this notion of speed, turnover or movement. Think of raw materials moving through a factory and becoming finished products, and think of those finished products moving off the shelf to the customer. That's asset velocity.

To make it easier to understand, think of one specific kind of asset: inventory. Picture a grocery store, in which the owner has made little investment in the shop itself and who sells for cash only. All the assets are in the form of inventory. Does the grocer empty her shelves and replace the goods each day, or does it take a week to clear the shelves? The first scenario has higher inventory velocity than the second. For many companies, including Ford, inventory velocity is a very revealing number.

Some people use the term "inventory turns" to describe inventory velocity. How many times does the inventory turn over in a year? Wal-Mart has 360 inventory turns in disposable diapers. That means the entire inventory of diapers is sold almost every day.

Figuring out the return on assets requires some simple arithmetic: your total sales for, say, a year divided by total assets (or total inventories in the case of inventory velocity). But forget the math. Get the **idea** of velocity. Things must move through a business to the customer — the faster the better.

How long is it from the time an order comes in to Ford Motor Company to the time it is delivered to the customer? How long from the time Ford receives raw materials and parts to the time finished product is being sold out of the dealers' showrooms? If you cut these cycle times by half, asset velocity doubles. The business thinking is making the commitment to double the asset velocity while, of course, keeping consumers happy. The leadership skill is in figuring how to do it and doing it ahead of the competition.

The faster the velocity, the higher the return. In fact, the return on assets is nothing more than profit margin multiplied by velocity, $R = M \times V$. It is stated as a percentage — 8 percent return, 10 percent return, 15 percent return — a single number that can be used for comparison. A businessperson is less

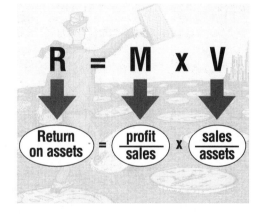

concerned about precision. She uses it to get a sense of the business. Is it better than last year and the year before that? Is it better than competitors'? Is it where it should be? The best companies have a return on assets greater than 10 percent after tax.

Making Velocity Meaningful

Many people focus on margin, but they overlook velocity. A true businessperson thinks about both.

Look at AT&T and Dell. AT&T's profit margin is around 12 percent after tax, up a little from 1997, but continually at risk. CEO Michael Armstrong has been working hard to find opportunities in voice, data, text and video. There's a lot of competition in telecommunications, and AT&T has a lot of fixed costs. The PC business is cutthroat, too. Dell's margin was only around 8 percent after tax for the year ending in February 1999.

Now look at velocity. AT&T has a very high fixed

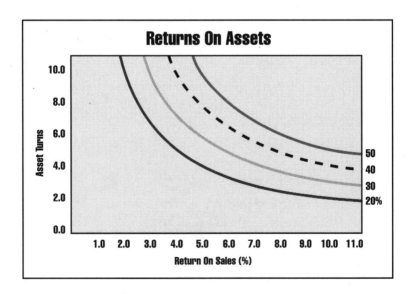

investment in plant, wires, distribution and switches. Its asset velocity is less than 1. Would a businessperson be concerned about that? You do the multiplication: 12 percent x 0.89, and you find that AT&T has a return on assets of around 11 percent.

Dell has relatively low fixed investments. Dell's return on assets is 28 percent. Its return on invested capital (the measure Dell uses) is a whopping 90 percent! (Accounts payable — the money Dell owes suppliers — has been deducted from assets but not from invested capital, thus the difference.) Dell didn't get there because of the margin. It got there because of the business thinking. Michael Dell figured out velocity.

What do you think Dell's inventory velocity is? It's 50. Michael Dell saw that other low-margin businesses, like grocery stores, were earning returns of around 3 percent to 4 percent. That got him thinking. Now senior executives of companies like United Technologies and Pratt & Whitney are visiting Dell. What are they doing at a PC company?

As you hone your business skills, think hard about return on assets and its basic ingredients. Look at Ford's return on automotive assets. It's about 5.4 percent after tax.

THE LANGUAGE OF SHAREHOLDER VALUE

Does the action create shareholder value?

Look at SVA profit:

$$\text{SVA profit} = \text{Net income} - [\text{Net operating assets} \times \text{Cost of capital}]$$

Net operating assets is net receivables, inventories, plant, property, equipment, tooling, and goodwill.

Why focus on these assets? Because they are the real drivers of the business — the assets requiring high returns to justify the risk associated with making the investment.

If you don't think 5.4 percent is adequate, press for ways to improve it. Even if you don't have all the answers, you can help by asking the right questions.

Where are the opportunities to improve Ford's return on assets? Take the return on small cars, which has been problematic for companies around the world. Some manufacturers have in fact been earning less than 2 percent return on assets on small cars, which is below the cost of capital. At that rate, the more small cars they sell, the more they destroy shareholder value.

How might that part of the business generate a higher return?

One truth about business is that the return on everything you've invested in has to be greater than the cost of using your own and other people's (bankers' and shareholders') money, the **cost of capital**. If your return is greater than the cost of capital, you have created value for shareholders.

Ford has begun to use SVA — shareholder value added — to keep this universal truth front and center. Ford's concept of SVA is designed to answer the simple but important question: Do profits exceed the return required by investors? "SVA profit" shows whether an action adds to shareholder value. SVA is the ultimate test of whether the money-making is adequate to keep investors satisfied.

Growth

How would you feel if your business wasn't growing? Is Ford growing? Far from management's expectations. Think of other big companies that are not fast growers. Sears. McDonald's. Do you remember Westinghouse? People used to compare it to GE. Westinghouse is gone. Recall Digital Equipment? It was one of the top computer companies in the world. Gone. Same with Atari.

> **Growth for its own sake doesn't do any good. Growth has to be profitable and sustainable.**

A good businessperson recognizes that no growth means lagging behind in a world that grows every day. If you don't grow, competitors will eventually overtake you.

If you do grow, you will energize the business.

Growth has a psychological dimension. A company that is expanding attracts talented people with fresh ideas. It stretches them and creates new opportunities. People like to hear customers say they're the best and that more business will be coming their way.

Growing the Right Way

But growth for its own sake doesn't do any good. Growth has to be profitable and sustainable. You want growth to have better margins and higher velocity — both compared with competitors. And growth has to use capital investment efficiently. SVA can tell you whether new business returns more than the cost of capital.

Have you heard of Harold Geneen, the CEO who turned ITT, once a $500 million telephone company, into a $19 billion conglomerate by buying almost everything in its path? By 1978 the company was huge. But when the buying spree ended, the return was unsatisfactory. The conglomerate went downhill from there and no longer exists.

So don't use size as a measure of success. Pushing for more sales dollars isn't necessarily good business. You have to know how and why you're growing. And you have to consider whether you are growing in a way that can continue.

Look at what is happening to your cash. Maybe sales are increasing but the cash situation is getting worse. Step back. Are you growing in a way that is generating or consuming cash? Is your profit margin improving or getting worse?

If the money-making is improving and the cash is

growing too, you have some interesting choices. You can use the funds to develop a new product, buy another company, or expand into a new country. Maybe you want to add some new features to make your product more appealing. Maybe you can cut the price and expand demand profitably. Part of Henry Ford's business acumen was in understanding that lower prices and higher wages would expand demand and contribute to money-making.

Growth Potential

Finding opportunities for profitable growth when others can't is part of business acumen. Sam Walton, the founder of Wal-Mart, knew how to grow a business, even when his industry peers thought it was impossible. In 1975, the CEO of Sears, Roebuck told a class at Northwestern's Kellogg School of Business that retailing in the U.S. was a no-growth industry. He said it was mature. Meanwhile, Sam Walton was opening new stores while maintaining a return of at least 35 percent.

In 1990, Sears was the world's largest retailer. Now Wal-Mart has that title. Even without its founder at the helm, Wal-Mart seems to understand growth. For the year ending January 31, 1999, Wal-Mart had sales of $137 billion, up $20 billion from the previous year. Sears' 1998 sales were $41 billion, about the same as in 1997. Wal-Mart is also more profitable than Sears.

Finding opportunities for profitable growth requires drive, tenacity and risk-taking. As Jac Nasser told the investment community in January 1999, Ford has been evaluating several avenues of growth and will pursue those that have the greatest potential to create value. Ford's growth options include using strong brands and great products to expand market share (the Jaguar S-TYPE and Ford Excursion, for example); positioning for geographic expansion, particularly for long-term opportunities in India, China, Thailand and other emerging markets; providing services in other aspects of car ownership, through Auto Collection, Kwik-Fit and Collision Team America, for instance; and exploiting synergies between our businesses and pursuing acquisitions and adjacencies.

Adjacencies is the word Jac Nasser uses to describe market segments that are different but closely related. When a consumer buys a vehicle, that person needs to finance it, insure it and, over time, maintain it and buy replacement parts. Financing, insurance, maintenance and parts are separate market segments, but they are closely related to the initial vehicle purchase. Over the life of the car, an average person spends $68,000 in total. How can Ford create shareholder value from participating in all these segments? How does Ford measure whether growth will be profitable? Quite simple really: The additional revenue (or sales) must generate positive SVA.

Customers

The street vendor has to know his customers. The same holds true in any business. It's universal. At Ford, you talk about the people who buy and use your products as **consumers** — who are the consumers and what are they buying? You don't talk about what you are selling. Can you see the difference in those two things?

You hear people talk about "the value proposition." That's not the language of a shopkeeper. Keep it simple. How simply can you describe what consumers are buying? It might not be the physical product alone. Maybe they're buying reliability or service. For the street vendor, it includes trustworthiness.

Let's use Sears again as an example. For many years, women shoppers were buying well-known brand names, yet Sears missed that trend completely. When Arthur Martinez became CEO in 1995, he began to change the product mix to try to pull the company out of the doldrums. Sears began to emphasize popular name brands and advertised the change in its product mix through its "softer side of Sears" campaign.

The street vendor interacts with consumers every day. He is focused on the reality of the business, not complex accounting measures. In large companies, too, you have to see beyond the financials. When you can't get the prices and margins you used to get, talk to consumers to understand why. Observe them directly, unfiltered, not through the eyes of the dealers.

Some people talk about customer loyalty. But you have to earn loyalty every time you come in contact with a customer. Consumers need a simple reason to buy from you. You have to give them something they really need. You can find out what they need — from them. You would be surprised how often this common sense of business is lacking.

CHAPTER 3

Ford's Total Business

Cash, return and growth can be measured with accountants' tools, but businesspeople don't memorize these words like terms in a textbook. They understand their real meaning, instinctively combine them and use them to create a mental picture of what is really happening in the business. A true businessperson combines the elements of money-making to get an intuitive grasp of the total business and what generates positive SVA.

A doctor's diagnosis is a simple comparison. Doctors take the pulse, the blood count, the temperature and the like. From simple measurements, they deduce what is happening with the body. Regardless of how many tests have been conducted, a good diagnosis requires judgment of the body's overall health. Is it improving or declining?

When Jack Welch announced a 13 percent increase in GE's earnings in July 1998, he said the result showed the company's ability to deliver "top-line growth, increased margins and strong cash generation." You can see the business thinking — cash, return and growth. GE's operating margin was 16.7 percent in 1998, up from 15.7 percent the year before. Sales rose 11 percent from 1997 to 1998, and the company generated $10 billion in cash.

Let's use an illustration closer to home. Henry Ford had an intuitive sense of how the total business made money. He not only made legendary breakthroughs in manufacturing but also reduced the price of a touring car every year from 1909 to 1915, and in 1914, introduced the $5 workday.

In 1916, the Dodge brothers, who owned a stake in Ford, filed a lawsuit because they wanted higher dividends. During the court case, the Dodge brothers' attorney challenged Henry Ford's statement that the purpose of the company was to "incidentally make money." "Incidentally make money?" the attorney asked Mr. Ford. "But your controlling feature is to employ a great army of men at high wages, to reduce the selling price of your car, so that a lot of people can buy it at a cheap price, and give everybody a car that wants one."

"If you give all that, the money will fall into your hands; you can't get out of it," Mr. Ford replied.

Do you think Henry Ford had fun making money? When I'm teaching classes at Ford and I ask how many people made money as a kid, lots of hands go up.

When I ask who had fun doing it, the room bursts with excitement. People get very nostalgic about those early experiences delivering newspapers or mowing lawns.

What's different now? You work for a money-making enterprise, but chances are you've had neither the information nor the opportunity to think like a businessperson. After going to school, you probably got channeled into a narrow specialty and kept your nose to the grindstone to try to become the best in that area. That's how you moved up and got rewarded.

The excitement will come back when you apply to Ford the universal law of business. What do you know about your own company?

Ford is huge and has a long history as a manufacturer of automobiles. It has four distinct businesses (Automotive,

Ford Credit, Visteon and Hertz), numerous manufacturing plants, and seven primary vehicle brands that are well known in many different countries (Jaguar, Aston Martin, Lincoln, Ford, Mercury, Mazda and Volvo).

These are the kinds of things a shopkeeper would know about his business, and they are common knowledge throughout Ford. But now the difference between the shopkeeper and most Ford managers emerges. See if you can answer the following questions:

☞ What were Ford Automotive's sales in 1998? They were $119 billion worldwide.

☞ Are they growing, declining or flat? They were down 3 percent from 1997. Before that, sales had been growing by 5 percent annually — but that growth was driven mostly by pricing increases, a thing of the past in the auto business. Is this growth picture good enough for a vibrant company?

☞ What is Ford's profit margin (return on sales)? Is it growing, declining or flat? The margin, after taxes, was about 4 percent in 1998. That's up slightly from 1997.

☞ How does Ford's margin compare with competitors'? It's higher than GM's and also higher than Toyota's last reported year-end result, but does 4 percent remind you of anything — say, a Wal-Mart or a grocery store?

☞ Do you know your inventory velocity? It's about 21. Sounds good, but there's a catch to it. "Inventory" on Ford Automotive's balance sheet consists of purchased parts, parts being worked on and assembled in the plant, and vehicles inside the factory. It does not include vehicles in transit between the plant and the dealer or on the dealer's lot. If we were to calculate a number combining those things, the inventory velocity would be much lower. Ford's automotive asset velocity is 1.4 — much lower than the best companies.

☞ What is Ford's return on assets? You can figure it out: asset velocity of about 1.4 x after-tax margin of 4 percent. Return on assets is about 5.4 percent. (Remember, Dell's is 28 percent.)

☞ Is cash increasing or decreasing? Cash has been increasing. It increased by $3 billion from 1997 to 1998. What did Ford do to generate cash?

Scrutinized capital investments more sharply and began working on inventory velocity.

☞ Are you gaining or losing against the competition? Losing in major markets. Ford's share of U.S. and European markets has declined every year since 1995.

☞ Is Ford considered high cost? Compared to the world's best, yes.

☞ Finally, is Ford creating shareholder value? SVA was $1.5 billion, best of the auto companies, but not as good as the best companies. Looking at returns to shareholders, since the end of 1996, the stock price has gone from $21 to a high of around $67, and Ford paid dividends and spun off Associates First Capital. Total return to shareholders has been in the top quartile. But so far this year (1999), it's below average.

Let's recap: sales of $119 billion, up nicely over the last five years but down from 1997. Market share declining in major markets. Considered high cost. Margin of 4 percent after-tax. Asset velocity of 1.4. Inventory velocity of 21 and increasing. Cash increasing. SVA positive. Providing

What can you say about Ford's total business?

Ford is on the move. In 1999, it has:

- **SVA positive and increasing**

- **High cost**

- **Low velocity**

- **Low return**

- **Flat or no growth**

- **Increasing cash**

What business questions must you ask?

What must you do?

top-quartile returns to shareholders over the last three years, but not so far this year.

Now you are speaking the universal language of business. You're getting a picture of Ford Automotive's **total business**, the kind a shopkeeper would have. And it didn't take a lot of numbers to get there — sales, margin, total inventories, assets and cash. You can pull the numbers out of the annual report, and you don't need pinpoint accuracy to understand the reality of Ford.

PART II

THE BIG-COMPANY DIFFERENCE

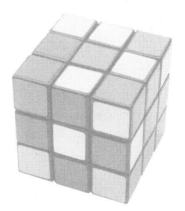

CHAPTER 4

The Rubik's™ Cube

The nucleus of Ford is the same as the street vendor's. But of course there are differences between a one-man shop and a huge corporation. Why do many successful small-company leaders flounder as their companies grow?

Some fall down on the people side. They don't know how to develop people and synchronize individuals' efforts as the staff increases. Many other business leaders falter simply because they can't deal with the complexity of a larger business. They can't cut through to the nucleus of the business and make the right judgment about which set of activities, or business priorities, will meet the money-making goals. They're overwhelmed, they can't decide, they can't prioritize, they lose focus, or they make the wrong judgment.

Think about the business challenge as a brain teaser. Maybe you're familiar with the toy called a Rubik's™ cube. Each side of the cube is divided into nine squares of six different colors. The idea is to twist and turn the cube until all the red squares are on one side, the yellows on another side, and so on. Unless you have an approach for solving the puzzle, you will go through countless combinations before you get to the right one.

A large company like Ford is like a giant Rubik's™ cube. There are internal things and external things to consider, each of which can vary. For each variable, there's the present status as well as projections about the future. It's as if the colors of the Rubik's™ cube could change!

Predicting and Creating Change

Think of what's happening in Ford's environment in 1999-2000. Ford is the second-largest industrial concern in the world, with about 400,000 employees and dozens of big competitors, from car manufacturers to major banks and credit unions, worldwide. Ford sells about 7 million vehicles each year (that's 20,000 a day) in 200 countries and territories and operates 179 plants on six continents. Each country has its own economic picture, currency, consumer trends, competitive dynamics and social concerns. Ford has seven primary vehicle brands and numerous nameplate brands, each of which has various options. Needless to say, the number of combinations and permutations is immense.

Exceptional businesspeople do what no computer can do. They scan the external environment, and out of all the things that are going on in the world, they are able to identify the significant patterns and trends.

They evaluate the business from many perspectives — regions, functions, product lines, brands, consumer segment — in order to improve their understanding of the business. It's like looking at all sides of the Rubik's™ cube at the same time.

It's not pure guesswork to predict that a new market will be created or a new need generated. After all, the future is created from what already exists. All the key technologies necessary for the PC existed in 1976. IBM, Xerox and Hewlett-Packard had working models. The seeds had been planted, yet Apple caught everyone off guard.

In 1995, few people were talking about deflation, but Jac Nasser was one of a handful of business leaders who concluded that deflation was coming. He considered various assessments of business and global economic trends and made an informed judgment.

Ford started preparing for a deflationary environment based on Jac Nasser's business sense of what would take shape. He realized before most that increasing prices in many product areas would be almost impossible to achieve. To improve margins, Ford would have to be tenaciously focused on productivity improvement, as would suppliers and partners. Some products and brands that were unlikely to provide a promising return and that required capital investment had to be eliminated.

Despite the complexity, a business leader must set the business priorities. What three or four business activities are most important? If the leader fails to set the priorities or keeps changing his mind, the whole organization loses energy. If, on the other hand, he sets the business priorities and communicates them clearly and often, people will have a better sense of what to do.

Business Acumen

The ability to conceive the total business in all its complexity and determine the "right" set of business priorities is the essence of business acumen. Some people are able to cut through the complexity and find an underlying logic that connects the business priorities and explains, in common sense terms, how the business will make money. What customers will they serve? What kinds of value will they provide? How will they gain an edge over the competition? How will the company achieve all the money-making goals simultaneously?

> ## Business Acumen =
>
> **The ability to determine the business priorities that achieve all the important money-making goals simultaneously (cash, ROA, growth and continuously increasing shareholder value).**
>
> **The timing, sequencing and speed of money-making actions affect shareholder value creation.**

Michael Dell's insight into velocity is a good example of business acumen. Think about it against the backdrop of cash, return, growth and customers. If Dell Computer could deliver PCs to customers in four days, customers would be pleased (customer satisfaction). Inventories would be low (cash freed up for more interesting things).

What else is good about low inventories? How about obsolescence of component parts — a huge issue in Dell's business? If you lower the obsolescence, there's less risk that the market will reject the things you produce. In high technology, prices of parts fall quickly. If the price declines each week, don't you want to take advantage of it to preserve your already slim margin? Margin improves, customers benefit. Michael Dell has the business acumen to see the logical connections between these things.

Or consider Jorma Ollila's business acumen. At a young age, he transformed Nokia from a sprawling conglomerate into the world's largest — and highly profitable — mobile phone company, displacing Motorola. Working backward from the consumer, Nokia designers converted the phone from a purely functional instrument to a fashion statement by reducing size and weight, adding style and introducing new features faster than anyone. Nokia made the brilliant move of participating in AT&T Wireless' one-price plan, thereby landing a huge customer. New products command a better price premium, large volume reduces costs, so you can reduce price and maintain margins, and short product cycles improve velocity. All create shareholder value.

You can find examples of business acumen at Ford.

From 1995 to 1998, total unit sales for North America rose only 1 percent, while revenue rose some 18 percent. That means that for every unit sold, Ford gets $2,700 more in revenue than it did in 1995. Profits have increased $3.5 billion during that period. The improvements were not just because of cost cutting and price increases: About 80 percent of the improvement was due to changing product mix.

Ford had the business acumen to identify vehicles with the greatest potential for profit (high-margin vehicles like the new Ford F-Series and Expedition and Lincoln Navigator) and channel its marketing and manufacturing resources to deliver the best value to consumers in those areas. The Ranger is a case in point. Since 1997, the mix of 4x4 sales has improved from 13 percent to 39 percent; the mix of super cabs has increased from 39 percent to an amazing 80 percent.

Ford Motor Company's purchase of Volvo, its purchase and subsequent turnaround of Jaguar, its successful refurbishing of Lincoln, and the recent creation of Premier Automotive Group under the leadership of Wolfgang Reitzle, who has the luxury-car DNA — all reflect Ford's business acumen to recognize and benefit from the increasing wealth of people around the world.

Another example of business acumen at Ford is the decision to launch the Navigator, using the Expedition platform and existing plant capacity. The Ford management team saw an opportunity to create a new nameplate brand for a new market segment. The business result? Superior growth, margin and velocity. In Jac Nasser's words, "Lincoln Navigator virtually created a new segment overnight and brought to Lincoln consumers who were totally new to the brand."

Or consider the Ford Production System, developed internally over the last three years. FPS is, in Jim Padilla's words, the backbone of how the plants will run. By reducing the time from when an order is received to when it is shipped, it generates cash and reduces inventories by an order of magnitude similar to Dell. It reduces waste, double-handling and space. At the same time, it satisfies customers better and therefore gives Ford the chance to improve market share and revenue growth. The goal is to be able to produce whatever the customer wants when he wants it. FPS is one of many initiatives under way that directly link to cash, return, growth and SVA.

Some CEOs succeed for a while because they can engineer mergers and acquisitions and weave persuasive stories for security analysts on Wall Street. They're known as deal-makers. But without business acumen, they don't last long. Once those other things get done, the person doesn't know what to do with the business. More than once I've heard directors say things like, "Sure, he understands Wall Street, but can he really run the business?"

Test Your Business Acumen: The AT&T Example

Imagine that you're standing in Michael Armstrong's shoes. It's the fall of 1997, and you're the new CEO of AT&T. Your margin is thin and getting thinner. Prices are declining. Velocity is 1. Fixed costs are huge. And there are some "interesting" things happening in the environment — data, wireless communications, cable, satellites, Internet, expansion of demand internationally, global megamergers. Upstart "dot-com" companies are getting created every day with exorbitant stock prices.

What is your judgment about which way these things are going? Do you have to change your business? Expand it? If so, what segments, what geographies? Do you go it alone or create joint ventures?

You're losing market share, and now small entrepreneurs are buying wholesale, selling retail and hacking down the price of long-distance calls. Could you acquire them? Maybe, but you would need some capital.

Do you need to find a new market to enter? You would have to know about legislation, the FCC, local laws and all kinds of technologies that are hard to keep track of. If you can't find those markets and grow faster than the other guys, couldn't your company be acquired by somebody else?

What about customers? There are two kinds of global customers. There's the kind like American Express, which operates all over the world, and there's the guy in Germany who wants local service. Does AT&T have what global markets want? What are the obstacles — in business school language, what are the "barriers to entry?"

The word that causes heartburn in this business is "Internet." What's the Internet going to do? Will people make calls on the Internet? If so, what could happen to AT&T's volume? What combination do we want? What do we need? We can't balk at change. That's not leadership. We have to use it as a vehicle to drive cash, return, growth and customers.

And you might ask, "Do we have the people who can answer these questions? And how much time should we give them?"

We have to make some assumptions. Then somebody asks, "What if you're thinking too short term and a new technology comes along?" What do we tell that person? Do we wait? Can we wait? You heard about the declining margin, low return on investment. What do you think is happening to cash flow? It can't be good.

Is your mind getting overloaded with the complexity of AT&T? Welcome to the executive suite! This is the complexity of any large business. As a leader, you cannot avoid complexity. Take a minute to decide where you would place your bets.

In mid-1998, Michael Armstrong and his team made the judgment that data, voice, text and Internet would be bundled, and they decided to reach consumers directly instead of going through local telephone companies. AT&T made two bold moves: It acquired TCI, and it entered a joint venture with Time-Warner. The energy began to flow, and the stock price rose 40 percent.

CHAPTER 5

How $1 Equals $30

There is one more complicating factor associated with big companies. If the company is large enough and decides to "go public," its money-making capacity can be greatly magnified.

Say I'm Mr. Black (a fictitious name). I run a big, publicly held company, which means many people own shares. At the end of the year, I have to issue an annual report telling how much profit I made. I did pretty well this year. For every share of stock in my business, I made $1 profit. So did my biggest competitor, Ms. White.

The price of my stock is $30. The price of Ms. White's stock is $38. My stock is worth 30 times more than the $1 I earned. Ms. White's is worth 38 times more. Now that's what I call unfair! We both made $1 a share, but one stock is worth much more than the other.

When the stock market goes up, our stock prices move up roughly in the same proportion. When the market goes down, they go down in the same proportion. In either case, my stock price is worse than hers.

> **For public companies, a dollar earned is not a dollar of value created. The stock market, an innovation of Western civilization, provides the opportunity to magnify wealth.**

What happens next year if my earnings per share go up by, say, 10 cents after tax? Providing the stock market doesn't go to the dogs, what should I expect my stock price to be? The market will multiply the $1.10 in earnings by 30. I can expect my stock price to be $33, a $3 increase.

As you can see, for public companies, a dollar earned is not a dollar of value created. The stock market, an innovation of Western civilization, provides the opportunity to magnify wealth.

Anyone who works for a public company must understand this phenomenon. Investors multiply a company's earnings by some number that reflects their overall confidence in the company's present and future money-making ability. That number is called a multiple, or a price-earnings ratio (P-E).

Don't be intimidated by the terminology. You already know what the "P" and the "E" are. People are willing to pay $30 for a share of Mr. Black's stock; this is the P, for stock price. He earned $1 per share; this is the E, for earnings. You put the P over the E, which means you divide 30 by 1. You don't need a calculator for this one: 30 divided by 1 is 30. That's the P-E ratio.

The GE Track Record

A higher multiple creates more shareholder value. If you took all the GE shares and multiplied them by the stock price, you would find that the company was worth a total of about $333 billion at the end of May 1999. GE has the world's second-largest market value (Microsoft, worth $412 billion, recently moved into the number one position). Three years ago, GE was worth less than $100 billion.

How did GE create so much value for stockholders in such a short time? By growing its operating margin, or earnings, and by doing things that boosted the multiplier of those earnings. In 1995, GE's multiple ranged from a low of 13 to a high of 19. In March 1999, it was around 37 — well above the average for all companies.

Look at what GE has been doing. It has delivered solid growth — sales growth of at least 6 percent a year (11 percent last year), operating margin improving every year, EPS (earnings-per-share) growth of 12 percent to 15 percent — for 17 years in a row. One of GE's measures of asset velocity, "working capital turns," went from 5.8 in 1995 to 9.2 in 1998. And the company generates cash, no accounting tricks.

When investors see that consistency over many years, they begin to think it will continue.

Investors are confident that GE has figured out a way to make consistently more money quarter after quarter, year after year. It's a money machine.

This is a very deliberate effort within GE. All GE employees know that if they can't contribute to the money-making, they should go to work for a company with a lower multiple. So cash, profitability and growth, and all the while meeting and anticipating customers' needs by helping them improve their processes — in short, business acumen — is in the genes of the people who stay and thrive at the company.

A public company that grows the top line and the bottom line — that is, gets more sales and increases the profit margin without lowering velocity — will increase the value of the stock. By how much? That depends on the multiple. And what happens to the multiple if you build confidence in the market over time? It rises.

The Multiplier Effect

So, making money is good. Creating the means to make consistently more money over time is better. Unless you take the multiplier effect into account, you  may be underestimating the rewards for business acumen as well as the punishments for lack of business acumen.

What happens if the company begins to miss, even by a penny? Stock prices fall sharply. Investors might wonder about your discipline and your ability to deliver on your commitments. Your multiple erodes, so even when you have a great quarter, your stock price doesn't move much. It isn't long before the CEO and the board of directors start to get phone calls from investors, some of whom manage these huge pension funds and mutual funds and own millions of shares. Executives have to produce results or they lose their jobs. The collective action of investors can be vicious when a company doesn't deliver.

What else could happen if the stock price sinks? People will say the company is underperforming. Maybe the CEO of another company will begin to think your stock is a bargain. He can now afford to buy you and will take on the task of improving the performance. Maybe your multiple is pretty high compared with your competitors but pretty low compared with companies outside your industry. Take it as a sign that people think your industry has little room for growth. Then challenge that no-growth assumption. Remember, Wal-Mart and Home Depot created great market value in so-called low-growth markets.

Now let's go back to Mr. Black and Ms. White. Most

likely they run their businesses differently. Not unlike arch rivals Coke and Pepsi, with multiples of 33 and 27, respectively. For about 10 years in a row, Pepsi's sales grew 14 percent every year, while Coke's sales grew 10 percent a year. But Coke made a bigger profit on its sales, and its return on investment was consistently higher. Sure, Pepsi was growing in terms of total sales, but Coke was doing a better job of meeting the various money-making goals. Investors noticed. Although Pepsi's P-E ratio rose a respectable 11 points (from 16 to 27), Coke's rose even more — 15 points (from 18 to 33).

Managing Ford's Multiple

If you know Ford's stock price and its earnings from operations, you can figure out its multiple. In 1996, it was 6. At the end of 1998, it was around 11. What does that say about the company? Do investors think the company is a growth company? Has the company consistently delivered?

Ford's multiple is substantially below that of major customers and suppliers and less than half of the S&P 500. Ford is being penalized for its low growth and its risk to a cyclical downturn.

To move the multiple higher, you have to convince investors that you have unleashed profitable new growth initiatives and that you have reduced your risk levels. You must demonstrate that you can increase profits consistently, year after year, and that you're the best in productivity improvement every year.

Say you find a vendor who will provide engineering services for $20 million less than you currently spend, after tax. Profits improve by $20 million. Using Ford's multiple of 11, the market value of the company increases by $220 million. Suppose you find ways to make improvements every quarter. If you keep working at it and the market begins to believe you can continue, why couldn't Ford's multiple go up to 20? It's not out of your reach. At a multiple of 20, an additional $20 million profit creates $400 million in shareholder value.

And who benefits besides shareholders? Employees, of course, who have opportunities to earn more, grow more, and at the extreme, avoid the uncertainty of changes imposed from the outside because the company has underperformed.

CHAPTER 6

Edge in Execution

Assume that you've determined three or four business priorities that hang together to create a powerful money-making machine. How will you actually get the work done in a company as large as Ford? You will need the help of other people to execute your business priorities.

To get tangible, measurable results consistently over time, you must be able to select and develop people, and you have to synchronize the efforts of those individuals. In addition to business acumen, you must demonstrate people acumen and organization acumen. You must be a leader of the business and of people.

In a small organization, everyone knows everything that's going on. They overhear each other on the phone,

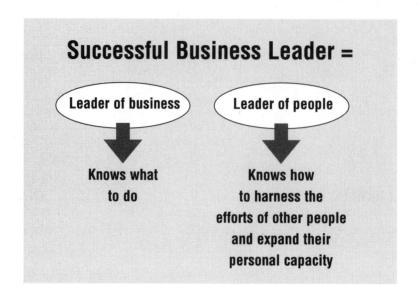

Successful Business Leader =

Leader of business → Knows what to do

Leader of people → Knows how to harness the efforts of other people and expand their personal capacity

they go to lunch. They automatically adjust to each other, make necessary trade-offs and synchronize their work. If there's confusion, they talk.

How do you get hundreds of people to work together in a larger organization? You create a structure. The moment you create structure, the social interaction in the organization, what you could call the **social architecture**, changes. Often, the information flows get clogged or distorted. It's harder for people to synchronize and adjust their work. This slows decision making.

In 1978, there were at least three people whose genius had not yet been discovered: Andy Grove, Gordon Moore and Bob Noyce. It was the beginning of Intel. Andy Grove ran the show when it was starting up in a garage and when it was a $20 billion giant. He learned to select and develop people, and he created a social architecture that kept the information flowing and got the work done as quickly. In his game, you don't last long if you can't make fast decisions. Intel has lasted. Andy Grove had an edge in execution.

Being a leader of people is important, but let's set something straight. Think of someone you consider to be a "people person." How would you describe him or her? When I ask that question at Ford, people come up with phrases like outgoing, well liked, lots of personality, enthusiastic, gets other people excited, charismatic.

> **Edge in Execution =**
>
> **Ability to deliver better, faster results through the efforts of other people.**

Personality alone is not what makes a company deliver. It takes insight into how the organization really works and how to link people's actions and decisions to the right things. It is this ability, in fact, that sets the superstar CEOs apart.

People Acumen

If you were Sam Walton and you were trying to build a business, how would you select people to run the new stores you're building? Making money in that business means managing margin and velocity and growing volume. If you can't figure out what kind of people can do that, forget about your dream of becoming bigger than Kmart.

Sam Walton had people acumen. He defined the most important criterion for hiring in his business: common sense. He carefully selected people who met the criterion and trained them. Employees were taught to watch sales, price, inventories and customers like a hawk. And they had autonomy to make decisions and take action.

The Right People

Every business needs the right people in the right jobs. Have you been to a Starbucks coffee shop? Did you notice its distinct ambiance? What about the people who make the coffee? This could be a boring job, but they seem to enjoy the experience. Starbucks seems to have a knack for attracting and selecting people who fit the ambiance. If Starbucks can't get those people and begins to deviate, don't you think fast growth could become a negative instead of a positive? You can't force-fit people into the job. The business suffers, and the people suffer.

Recently, Ford has been hiring a lot of senior people from other companies. Almost a third of Ford's officers have now been brought in from the outside because they have competencies that Ford needs right now — in brand management, for example. Also, many of them have run successful businesses and therefore have broad business acumen. These people will help Ford make the shift to a consumer-oriented company. They are key to Ford's ability to grow and create shareholder value. Won't everyone at Ford have greater opportunities if the business grows?

People acumen also includes discovering the best talent (the "A" players) and matching people to the job. Think about the person's aptitude and attitude. Make sure you're getting the right mind-set.

What's the mind-set of a traditional plant manager if he's used to two inventory turns and you say you're going to 30 turns? What happens if he resists the idea? We've all seen people who agree to things in meetings then go out the door and do nothing. If you have many of those kinds of people, what happens to the company's ability to execute?

> **People Acumen =**
>
> **A knack for selecting the right people, expanding their capacity and dealing with mismatches.**

What happens when a person is no longer matched to the job? A business leader has to face up to the mismatch and cut losses or the whole business suffers. Dealing with mismatches pronto and cutting your losses is another part of people acumen. Yet it is the bane of many businesspeople, including many prominent CEOs I've known. Over the years I've asked many CEOs what is the greatest mistake they've ever made in the area of people. The most common answer? "Waiting too long."

People who do well in the job also need attention. A true leader of people expands their capacity by helping them channel their skills, develop their abilities and release their positive energy. Expanding capacity may mean giving the person a "stretch job" that will force him to develop a new skill or gain a new perspective. It also means giving the person constructive feedback.

Maybe you think you give people feedback when you do their annual performance review. In reality, performance reviews are rarely used to develop people. Most of the time, they're simply a way to communicate a salary change based on last year's performance. That is not people acumen.

How would you feel if someone gave you positive feedback on the things you're doing well and specific suggestions for building your skills? Chances are you would feel that you had a personal coach, someone who wanted to help you succeed. You would feel energized. I can tell you from experience that it works. You can do it for those who report to you, and in the process, you will expand your personal capacity.

> **To succeed as a leading consumer company, Ford needs a diversity of people who reflect the consumer base and can look at a business situation through a variety of lenses.**

To succeed as a leading consumer company, Ford needs a diversity of people who reflect the consumer base and can look at a business situation through a variety of lenses. Ford is undertaking a major drive to expand the capacity of people of, for example, all genders, races and geographies. Diversity will help generate fresh insights, improve the quality of decision making, and help Ford stay attuned to the market.

Organization Acumen

Even if you have people acumen, you might not have an edge in execution. Talking about individuals does not fully capture the reality of an organization. Draw on your experience. What's missing? All the stuff that connects people to each other.

At most companies, much of the work gets synchronized and integrated in meetings. But as a mechanism, most meetings are weak. The wrong people attend, the dialogue is lousy, there's no leadership, no decisions get made, there's no follow through. Sometimes meetings are used to display a deck of useless slides. Sometimes they become a forum to blame people for not doing the right things.

So what's a better way? Do the work on the business side first, set the priorities, then design mechanisms that get the information flowing and the right people talking. These "integrating mechanisms" can be as simple as a conference call or a 15-minute meeting.

GE regularly uses conference calls for "Quick Market Intelligence." GE has even developed certain guidelines for making QMI calls effective: Questions should be specific and simple enough to answer in two minutes; all participants should be put at ease and encouraged to contribute; meetings should be short, so people don't lose interest; information should be processed along the way and summarized at the end. Following one such conference call, a GE scheduler, several layers removed from the vice president of manufacturing, felt comfortable calling the VP directly instead of going through the formal hierarchy. Communication was flowing; boundaries were breaking.

Wal-Mart's Strategy

Sam Walton created an integrating mechanism for which I think he deserves a Nobel Prize in Business (if there were such a thing).

Every Monday and Wednesday, 30 regional managers go out to visit nine Wal-Mart stores and six of their competitors' stores. They gather a basket of goods and compare the prices. In 1991, Wal-Mart had a policy about having prices that were 8 percent lower than major competitors in the area, and this was a way of checking.

> **Remember consumers. Who are they and what are they buying? Is it sustainable for the future? You assess this through competitive analysis.**

What are the regional managers observing if they're doing the job right? Not just prices. They're seeing the merchandise, how it is presented, what people are buying, what the stores look like, what the ambiance is, what new practices competitors are using, and they're watching employees.

Go back to the fundamentals. Remember consumers. Who are they and what are they buying? Is it sustainable for the future? You assess this through competitive analysis, which for Wal-Mart was going on constantly.

How many layers of people are there between the regional managers and where the action is? Zero. What is the value of zero layers of information? Time and quality. Zero delay. Zero filters. Zero distortion. And what is happening to the honing of the senses? The skill improves with practice.

The Results

On Thursday mornings, Sam Walton conducted a four-hour session with a group of the managers. Maybe it comes out in the Thursday morning meeting that one region needs a hundred thousand more grosses of sweaters on the shelf by Tuesday. By the way, those sweaters are not moving in the Northeast. It's not cold enough or whatever. Maybe inventory is getting adjusted.

> **Organization Acumen =**
>
> **Ability to synchronize the efforts of other people and link them to the business priorities.**

Information is being exchanged and integrated, decisions are made, and every participant is getting a total picture of the marketplace that is no more than 1 week old. People are acting on unfiltered information gathered directly from consumers and front-line employees.

Sam Walton's integrating mechanisms brought his priorities to the 50-foot level where the synchronization had to take place. At the same time, the accountability was built in. If someone wasn't readily participating in the meeting, it was very visible. Meanwhile, the mechanism helped create openness and trust.

Wal-Mart is truly a consumer-oriented company. But the point is not to copy Wal-Mart's integrating mechanisms. You have to detect for yourself where information sharing and trade-offs are critical and design mechanisms that are right for Ford.

Here's an example: About nine months ago, Ford's Business Leadership Implementation — Drive for Results created special teams to integrate people across functional chimneys. Each team is organized around a product, such as the Taurus, F-150, Econoline or Windstar, and includes people from purchasing, product development, marketing, manufacturing and finance. Team members pool their information and perspectives to identify two or three important items the team can work on together. Ideas are exchanged directly among the people who actually get the work done.

Designing specific integrating mechanisms isn't always easy, but it's important, and it's a leadership task, not a human resources task. Use your creativity and sharpen your organization acumen.

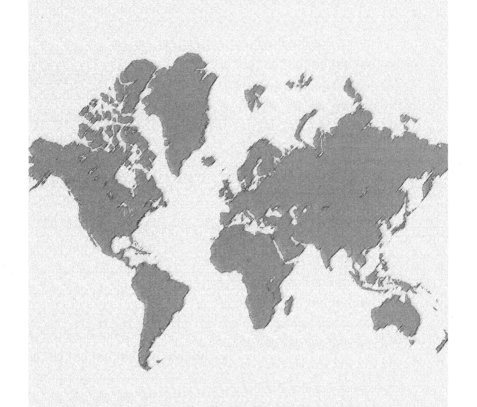

Ford Motor Company

PART III

PUTTING BUSINESS ACUMEN TO WORK AT FORD

CHAPTER 7

What Ford Needs to Do

By now you should be speaking the universal language of business. No matter where you are as a manager in Ford, you should have a shopkeeper's view of Ford's total business and be wrestling with the inherent complexity. You should also have an appreciation for how money-making is magnified by the stock market. Now you must cut through the complexity and apply your common sense to the business.

In 1994, Ford 2000 was introduced, which made Ford more efficient and responsive. The leadership team focused on productivity, quality and efficiency, and you got the payoff. Operating margins have improved each quarter for the past 14 quarters.

A lot of shareholder value has been created in recent

years. Return to Ford shareholders in 1998 was 89 percent, on top of 57 percent in 1997. Shareholder value increased in that period by more than $50 billion, and Ford has been in the top 15 outperformers in percentage terms on the New York Stock Exchange. So you can imagine where Ford was two years ago.

Despite these achievements, investors don't view Ford as a growth company or as a consumer company. So there are challenges. Everyone at Ford should know where Ford wants to go from here.

Ford is going for the third straight year of improvement in shareholder returns, and the goal is to be in the top 25 percent of the S&P 500 companies consistently over time. Achieving that goal means working especially hard on the fundamentals of return (margin and velocity), cash flow and growth, which will translate into a higher P-E multiple. This means increasing SVA each year. Ford's P-E multiple has nearly doubled in the past two years. The next challenge is to double it again. Why not? Even then it will be below the average of the S&P 500.

Many people think of Ford as a manufacturing company. But $144 billion worth of Ford products and services were sold to consumers last year. Unless Wal-Mart takes over, Ford is the second-largest seller of consumer products in the world.

A Consumer Company

The future lies in thinking of Ford as a consumer company. That must be the central thrust. You must think and act like a consumer company that provides automotive products and services. After all, consumer companies like Colgate and Unilever UK have P-E multiples of 35 and 23, respectively (as of March 1999). Ford's is 11.

> **The future lies in thinking of Ford as a consumer company. That must be the central thrust.**

Part of becoming consumer oriented is ensuring that each brand has a distinct identity that is widely communicated and understood. Do you know what each of Ford's brands represents? Every leader at Ford should. Positive brand image translates into true Ford enthusiasts and repeat purchases of Ford products and services. Ford has to continually identify and aggressively pursue promising opportunities to leverage its businesses and its brands for growth.

What is a Luxury Car?

"When the owner of a luxury car looks at his car in the parking lot, he is proud of its design, compared with the other cars in the lot. The car looks fast standing still. The proportions are like a sculpture. The front overhang is as short as possible; otherwise, the car will not look sporty. The wheels and tires fill the wheelhouse, so as not to give the impression of a sheet metal box on top of a chassis. The surface structure of the body has to be streamlined, shiny and taut like the muscles of a well-trained athlete. The gaps have to be parallel and as small as possible. The doors and seals have to be perfectly executed.

"Now, the owner opens the door. The handle signals the quality of the whole car. And when the door closes, it sounds like a vault. The seat and the interior fit like a tailor-made suit. Ergonomics are logically right. The owner feels in control like the pilot of a jet plane. Everything signals quality — high touch, high feel. The lines of the interior are flowing and generate a certain cocooning effect.

"When the car is moving, the engine sound is restrained. It is not loud or noisy but signals power and confidence. There are no squeaks, rattles and no boom. Only the powerful notes from the engine growing with acceleration.

"The feedback from the road is always responsive and

simultaneously comfortable. It's the opposite of a rolling sofa or a hay wagon with wooden wheels. The vehicle is agile, and for me, the idea is almost to create a car that behaves like an extension of each individual driver.

"What it boils down to is that you cannot just use facts and figures to compare luxury cars. It is a feeling and emotion combined with the harmonious product experience. Much of it cannot be designed by computer, and much of it is difficult to copy. The art of putting it all together is the unique domain and secret of 'the best.'

"Let me talk about the business of luxury cars. To be really successful with premium brands, you have to fine tune the entire process chain, from product development to customer service in a way that all fits together nicely and creates a consistent image and experience for each brand. It's a holistic approach.

"Continuity and consistency are important. You cannot jump around and create breaches in the integrity of the brand. Focus on quality, reliability and styling. Execute them at the highest possible level of perfection. You must create an obsession for perfection.

"Designing luxury cars and running the luxury-car business better than others requires solving trade-offs in a way that leads not to compromises but to optimization.

"To become the best luxury car company in the world, we have to become what I call an 'and' company. We have to have roominess AND compactness, high performance AND good fuel economy, distinctive design AND low aerodynamic drag, lots of features AND low weight, comfort AND sportiness, high-value design AND low development cost, AND ... AND ... AND ...

"In solving these contradictions better than others, we get to our ultimate goal: high prices AND high volume ... high profits AND high shareholder value."

— Wolfgang Reitzle, quoted in "Let's Chat"
May 14, 1999

Ford has the potential to sell a million luxury vehicles worldwide. Do you understand the essence of a luxury car?

Ford continues to make progress in becoming consumer focused. Entering adjacent segments, like Kwik-Fit, helps Ford interact with consumers several times over the life of a vehicle. Linking with consumers repeatedly builds relationships and helps Ford learn what new needs are emerging. Of course, each investment in an adjacent segment must create shareholder value on its own, but the major purpose is to help Ford become more consumer connected and consumer oriented.

A Good Corporate Citizen

Trust is the cornerstone of Ford's global brand strategy. To build trust, Ford has to be a good corporate citizen everywhere the company operates.

For a long time, Ford Motor Company has contributed to and cared about the communities where it operates. Now, the Spirit of Ford charge is to measure and demonstrate progress on social issues, as well as in business.

Ford Strategy Pyramid

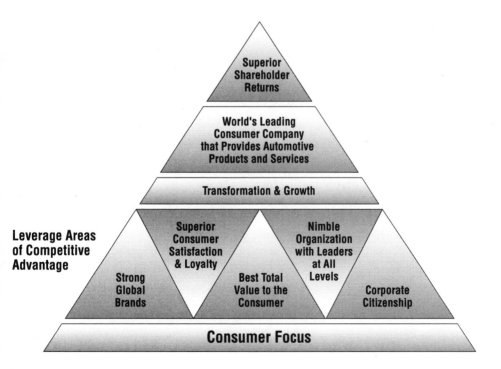

Consumers increasingly expect it, and businesspeople must realize that serving consumers also requires serving the broader needs of society, supporting sustainability of communities and cultures around the world. This builds trust.

This shows a commitment to listen and respond to the consumer. This demonstrates integrity.

> **Businesspeople must realize that serving consumers also requires serving the broader needs of society, supporting sustainability of communities and cultures around the world.**

Ford Motor Company must continue to be a leader on environmental and safety issues and a partner in local communities. It must deliver vehicles with higher value and fewer social trade-offs. Ford's strategy for being a good corporate citizen, "Cleaner, Safer, Sooner," is moving Ford in that direction. The creation of an Environmental Committee of the board of directors is another indication of Ford's commitment in this area. But consumers are the ultimate judges.

A Creator of Value

Building consumer loyalty has a definite impact on margins. Marketing costs are reduced, because the consumer needs less convincing through promotions and advertising. Revenues also will improve, because a trusted brand has psychological value to the consumer (as long as the perception and the reality are the same).

Ford wants to deliver the best total value to consumers, so you have to continue to improve productivity, efficiency and flexibility. Ford's productivity should be in the top 10 percent of all global manufacturing companies. You have to reduce the investment per dollar of sales, increase inventory velocity and be vigilant in lowering costs. You've achieved $5 billion in cost reductions over the last two years. The plan is to continue those efforts. You also have to view costs more broadly, through the consumer's eyes. You have to consider the total cost of owning a vehicle, which includes things like maintenance and insurance. How can Ford help in those areas?

Ford will create shareholder value by adopting a consumer mind-set and improving its global brands, customer satisfaction, corporate citizenship, total value and leadership. This is the simple statement captured in the "strategy pyramid" that appears in the 1998 annual report and has been circulated among the leadership team and the investment community.

Break the Barrier

A consumer mind-set changes the way Ford works. Achieving profitability and growth targets within each business — Ford Automotive, Ford Credit, Visteon and Hertz — requires working across functional chimneys. And delivering the best total value from the consumer's viewpoint means pursuing synergies across Ford's businesses. Barriers of hierarchy, function and business unit are things of the past.

Master the essence of Ford's business. How do you improve margins in an overall flat pricing environment? By using insight into the consumer to focus on high-margin products and services and by reducing the time it takes to launch new products, so you gain profitable market share earlier. You also have to buy smarter, which means you have to focus on global sourcing and developing productive partnerships with suppliers, which account for some 50 percent of total cost. You have to beat the Japanese at productivity improvement, reduce the break-even point, reduce fixed costs and fixed investment. If you make these improvements sooner and better than competitors, you will gain market share and generate cash.

If you provide better value and leverage your brands, sales will grow. Ford Motor Company gets less than 25 percent of consumer expenditure over the total life of a vehicle. By entering adjacent market segments, Ford's growth can accelerate. If you keep capital investment and fixed costs down as you grow, margins will improve. Keep asking, "Do we need to invest in fixed assets, or is there a better way?"

In 1999 Ford will invest $8.5 billion. If you reduce investment by half a billion every year over five years, you would accumulate $2.5 billion in cash. You also cut depreciation expense, so you improve margins. The $2.5 billion, invested elsewhere, could further improve margins and could lower your break-even and reduce risk.

Let's look at an example. You want to reduce inventory by $1 million, but you'll have to spend $50,000 after tax for premium freight. How do you know if that's wise? Subtract $50,000 from current profit, reduce current inventory by $1 million, then recalculate SVA. If SVA is better, shareholder value should improve. Indeed, at Ford's 10 percent after-tax cost of capital, the decision to reduce inventory and pay for premium freight would increase SVA profit by $50,000.

Better margins boost return on assets. But let's not forget about velocity. Doubling velocity will generate tremendous cash and improve the return. Cash, growth and return will improve the multiple and enable you to make sensible acquisitions. The bottom line is improved SVA and a better return for shareholders.

CHAPTER 8

How You Can Contribute

Each of you has a role to play in creating more shareholder value, regardless of your position or functional area. For example:

■ Human resources can help people break out of their chimneys and coordinate efforts with people elsewhere in the company. It can help ensure that Ford has the right people in the right jobs. The wrong person in the job can have a tremendously damaging effect on cash, velocity, growth and SVA.

■ Information technology needs to create links with customers and suppliers so you can collaborate more easily.

■ The office of the general counsel has to keep us up to

date with legislative changes globally. Do such changes create new opportunities?

■ Finance can help with many kinds of decisions — whether to add capacity, how to improve pricing for better margins and the like — by providing accurate and timely information. It can also be a partner in analyzing the most promising growth opportunities within and across the businesses. Finance is, in fact, well positioned to help cross boundaries, because it is already in so many areas of the business. Many finance people are at the right junction of information flow and can identify the important decision points. They can help speed Ford's progress.

Reframe the Issue

As your perspective expands beyond a functional or departmental view to a total business view, be creative. Maybe you can break new ground by reframing an issue and bringing underlying assumptions to the surface and challenging them.

What does it mean to reframe an issue?

Say you have a mandate to cut costs for new-model

Lincolns. You might begin a discussion by finding the facts about what consumers like or dislike about the car. If limousine drivers complain that the new model has a smaller trunk and poor lighting in the back seat, you might begin to wonder if cutting costs would make consumers less satisfied. If you can't change the price point, what can you do?   Maybe you're spending too much on things consumers don't value.

But wait. Broaden the discussion. Maybe cost is the wrong focus. What about volume?   If you improve the lighting and the trunk size, will you attract more buyers? If the margin drops from 11 percent to 10.5 percent but volume increases, you use capacity more fully. Are you better or worse off from a total money-making view? What happens to cash, return, growth and value of the brand? Are you creating shareholder value?

> **The goal isn't necessarily to have the greatest return — it's to create the greatest shareholder value.**

Can suppliers be part of the solution?   What other market segments are you missing? Is there a way to reduce cost and increase volume at the same time?

Keep in mind that the goal isn't necessarily to have the

greatest return — it's to create the greatest shareholder value.

Be Innovative

Look for innovative ways to improve the business. Some young people from purchasing have been exploring ways to take advantage of e-commerce. Using the Internet, they gathered a tremendous amount of data and sent detailed specifications to some suppliers around the world. They got 2,500 bids, from which they were able to choose the most competitive — all within 45 minutes. The process cut costs by more than 20 percent. This is the kind of experimentation and business thinking that will make Ford more competitive. As the velocity of innovation increases, you must unleash your creativity to make Ford more competitive.

Generate Ideas

You have been asked to read this book because you are a leader in your profession. By now, I hope you are convinced that professional excellence alone is not sufficient. To be a leader, you must be a businessperson first. You have to think like the street vendor and figure out how you can contribute to Ford Motor Company.

How can you, as a leader (keeping in mind cash, return, growth and customers) improve business and shareholder value? Ford employees are fired up. How can you tap every individual's intellectual energy?

Keep in mind the external realities: industrywide excess capacity, industry consolidation, flat pricing because of cutthroat competition, volatility of currencies, and the need to protect the environment and be a good corporate citizen.

Before you read on, use the blank space provided to make a list of ideas or priorities that can help. Apply your common sense. You will be surprised how many good ideas you can generate.

Write your ideas here:

Your ideas (continued):

Be a Leader

Don't let hierarchy and chimneys get in the way of understanding the essence of Ford's business. Every employee should have access to the same universal language and way of understanding the business. One great source of information is Jac Nasser's weekly letters. You've asked for it in the responses you give to those weekly letters. Use it in the meetings you have with people from other chimneys.

If you need to know more, ask questions.

Be a leader of the business. Pick the three or four items you and those reporting to you should focus on. Don't try to cover the waterfront, don't keep changing your mind, and don't back away from the challenge. Make the priorities known by repeating them often.

> By expanding your own capacity and the capacity of those around you, you will help Ford succeed. When Ford succeeds, you do too.

Be a leader of people. Find the right people for the job and take personal responsibility for releasing their energy and developing their skills. When someone's aptitude or attitude is impeding execution, address the issue. Don't forget to help others develop their own business acumen. By expanding your own capacity and the capacity of those around you, you will help Ford succeed. When Ford succeeds, you do too. You are an owner as well as an employee.

Be a leader of the organization. Link people's efforts to the business priorities. Find mechanisms that increase the information flow and synchronize people's work. Build the team.

Be a leader in your community and work to align Ford Motor Company's progress with that of the places you live and work. Take Henry Ford's advice: Live in a community, not on it.

Take Action

Start at the beginning. Return to your earliest experience in business, when you understood the nucleus of delivering newspapers or selling potholders or whatever it was you did to make money. Expand on your business acumen by practicing it in more complex situations. Don't be afraid to make mistakes and learn from them. Make judgments that reflect business acumen, and share your knowledge.

You have to decide what Ford must do and what it must stop doing. You have to determine the business priorities, and those priorities have to be consistent

> **You have to determine the business priorities, and those priorities have to be consistent and aligned with the corporate goals.**

and aligned with the corporate goals. You can't have too many, you can't keep changing, and you have to communicate them clearly and repeatedly. If your business acumen is any good (of course you'll keep improving it), you'll understand why that particular combination of business priorities will make money and result in improved shareholder value.

Don't get swept up in grandiose visions of what you want to accomplish. Bring the vision below the 50,000-foot level. You should be able to explain what you need to do in clear, simple terms, and you should be able to explain how it will improve money-making and create shareholder value.

Some of you may have the intellectual capacity to cut through complexity, but you're indecisive or afraid of being wrong. Can you wait until all the facts are in and the picture is clearer? Here's the rub: You make a bet even when you don't make a bet! That is, by not choosing to do anything different, you are choosing the status quo. Have the courage and conviction to provide focus for your area.

Don't let this book become an intellectual exercise. Before you close the cover, start thinking in concrete terms. Be prepared to answer the inevitable question: What are you going to do to help Ford's money-making in the next 60 to 90 days and improve SVA? Be a part of it. Let the excitement begin.

ACKNOWLEDGMENTS

My deep thanks to Jac Nasser, whose leadership and business acumen make great things possible.

Also, among the team at Ford Motor Company, I thank David Murphy, William Swift, Jim Padilla and Al Ver for serving as mentors in the development and completion of this book.

Jeff Guyton, Rob Kleinberg and Howard Welsh were tireless in their efforts to explain SVA in an approachable style and in developing the book's contents for a Ford audience.

Mel Stephens, Mike Parris, Ed Miller, Margaret Mellott, Kathy Yonkers, Matt Fillinger and Donna Vinikour marshaled this book through design, editing, approvals and production.

I would like to thank Geri Willigan for her great and creative contributions to this book. Also, my thanks to John Joyce and Noel and Patty Tichy for their constructive feedback and support over many years, and to Leonard Hill and Gary D'Lamater for their contributions to this project. Comments from Chris DeRose, Charlie Burck, Mike Foxx and Jim LiaBraaten also were helpful.

— Ram Charan

About Ram Charan

Ram Charan is an adviser to top management at Ford. He has long been an adviser to CEOs and senior executives of several other Fortune 100 companies. Current clients include General Electric Company, DuPont, Citigroup, and Universal Studios. His specialty is using reality-based approaches that help leaders link strategy and organizational behavior and convert vision into action for bottom-line results. He works with companies to develop differentiated and practical global strategies, design integrating mechanisms to improve decision cycle time and productivity, and build cross-functional, cross-cultural teams. He also advises CEOs on succession planning and using the board of directors for competitive advantage.

Formerly on the faculty at Harvard Business School and Northwestern University, Charan has won best teacher awards at Northwestern, Wharton School's Life Insurance Institute and General Electric. *Business Week* named him the number two resource for in-house corporate executive development programs in the United States.

Charan is the author of two highly acclaimed books: *Boards at Work* and, with Noel M. Tichy, *Every Business Is a Growth Business*. He has contributed several articles to the *Harvard Business Review*, including "Speed, Simplicity, Self-Confidence: An Interview with Jack Welch" (with Noel Tichy) and "How Networks Reshape Organizations — For Results." He is a frequent contributor to *Fortune* magazine: "Why CEOs Fail," "Managing Through the Chaos," "Two on Top," and "The Rules Have Changed" are among his contributions. His articles have also appeared in *Time, Information Week, USA Today, Leader to Leader, Director's Monthly, Directorship* and *The Corporate Board*.

Charan holds D.B.A. and M.B.A. (High Distinction and Baker Scholar) degrees from the Harvard Business

School. He is on the board of directors of Austin Industries in Dallas and on the Editorial Review Board of the Human Resource Planning Society.

He is based in Dallas, Texas. His e-mail address is *charanasoc@aol.com*.